I Didn't Mean to Forget

By Christine Vovakes

BLUE LIGHT PRESS • 1ST WORLD PUBLISHING

1ST WORLD
PUBLISHING

SAN FRANCISCO • FAIRFIELD • DELHI

Winner of the 2018 Blue Light Poetry Prize
I Didn't Mean to Forget

1st World Library
PO Box 2211
Fairfield, IA 52556
www.1stworldpublishing.com

Blue Light Press
www.bluelightpress.com
bluelightpress@aol.com

Book & Cover Art & Design
Melanie Gendron
melaniegendron999@gmail.com

Cover Photo
Christine Vovakes

Author Photo
Michael Vovakes

First Edition

ISBN 978-1-4218-3627-0

I Didn't Mean to Forget

CONTENTS

Measuring 1

Pauper's Blessing 2

Bill 3

Prayer in the Late Hours 4

Lost Lullaby 5

Grow Back 6

The Last Grains of Mazatlan Sand 7

Flood Gates 8

Two Brothers 9

To the Male Nurse Who Bathed Me 10

I Didn't Mean to Forget 11

Still Waiting 12

Encore 13

Braiding 14

Subterranean Spring 15

The Secret Behind Mona Lisa's Smile 16

After Phillip Moved 17

Mid-Life Blackout 18

Apple 19

Another Chance 20

A Condensed History 21

About the Author 23

Measuring

Complicated, how little we know
of each other, wanting the other's heart
to be a map, a place marked,
its distance to our own easily measured.

Instead, a swamp, thick reeds
and low-hanging Spanish moss
thwart progress. Clouds mask the sun,
filter light. I have no compass.

Somewhere ahead, you guide your skiff
through lily pads. I hear your oar dip in and over.
Later, if the moon slips through, she'll turn
your narrow wake into a silver thread

and I'll see clearly the distance between us.

Pauper's Blessing

Hunger, yes. It pries the hand open.
The palm outstretched receives crumbs
and calls them a meal.

Abundance is whittled
from crusts of bread,
that deep-down gnawing to be fed,

to open your mouth and share,
tongue to tongue, the morsel that love
makes into feast.

Bill

I want to remember him
a cowboy one day, a poet the next.
Editor of a small town newspaper,
he jousted at city hall windmills
sometimes when he wasn't quite sober.

He put a camera in my hand,
and a pen. And I gave him stories
that lit up the "People Page"
with the obscure and the unnoticed,
the septuagenarian boot maker
who only used leather that was
"soft as a woman's breast."

Bill loved my work.
Might have loved me.
A friend in the truest sense.

He anchors a headstone now.
No goodbyes.
He drifted off like chimes
growing more and more still.

And then silent.

Prayer in the Late Hours

That there will be time for us
to smooth
the love-rumpled bed;

time to create the day
with its yellow eye blinking
in a drift of lacy clouds.

Time to plant hyacinths and the fig tree,
time to crack open the pomegranate,
crunch the red bitter seeds.

Time to dig up the forgotten bones
that dream their way into waking
and whisper, "We never left."

Lost Lullaby

The ditch swims with moon,
watery-white
like breast milk for my newborn.

The years eclipse that moment
of mothering. I reclaim it,
though shunted aside years ago,

those midnights in the rocking chair
nursing my firstborn,
my son, moon sluicing down,

spilling through the window
with an ablution that even now,
in his hard middle years, blesses.

Grow Back

What's left but bone?

Desiccated lips,
and the heart flutters —
a dry acacia pod,
its seeds rattling in a twist of wind.

Let them land in damp soil,
sink into dark loam
and root.

From the warm rot
rise,
small green thing.

Fragile survivor,
give me a name.

The Last Grains of Mazatlan Sand

That song I mean the one about all of us—fiercely
irrelevant and yet so briefly alive
              — David St. John, *Generation*

Mazatlan blue washes sea and sky.
Between the airport and city
wildflowers surprise the dusty roadsides
pocked with wooden shanties, some leaning precariously,
missing boards and parts of metal roofs.

People missing too on that stifling drive
until we reach the city center suddenly thriving
with tourists in Nike shorts and tank tops,
yellow sundresses and big-brimmed straw hats.

Laughter and cold beer, tequila shots with lime;
music echoes from one condo complex to the next
down the sandy curve of coast.

The hot afternoon turns to balmy evening.
No worries here; poverty neatly hidden.
The sweet easy smiles of waiters, housekeepers,
the driver of the rickety cab who doesn't give a thought
to seat belts or air bags.

Those beautiful brown faces greet
the hungry, the lonesome, with warm welcomes
as open as the cantina's wide door.

There's nothing to do here but *be*:
dance, swim, dive in the sun.
spill your heart out and don't care where it falls.

Flood Gates

Like rivers flooding their banks,
we are surging, amorphous water
contained by boundaries constantly changing,
channeling through granite
a story told in shifting patterns.

Or a lake that takes
in the darkness a reflection
of the moon, repeating
the thin reeds and ghostly lotus
that grow above the water
and double themselves
on the mirrored surface.

Alone, we are a fraction
of what we seem, needing others
to give us shape and name,
slosh our sediment from slumber,
nudge our voice from slow, dumb stones.

I who have been rill
and brook and raging sea
settle into silence, a watery body of waiting,
the still pond your hand swirls.

Two Brothers

for Vincent and Donal

One needs a kidney, the other,
even after major heart surgery, says

"Take mine. Tests will show
we're compatible."

As indeed they were
all their lives,

one in Ireland, the other in California,
loving fiercely through the distance

one willing to give the shirt off his back,
the other, marrow from his bones.

To the Male Nurse Who Bathed Me

First day of vacation in Santa Cruz:
a slip, a shattered hip,
surgery in an unfamiliar hospital.
The painful wakening, the stuttering leg
that could not walk or bear weight.
The nightmare-inducing Vicodin,
the morning oatmeal, the evening stew,
the lonely midnight tears,
and through it all, like Blanche DuBois,
my total dependence on the kindness of strangers.

You were one of them, appearing my last day
before transfer to rehab,
my dark hair a long matted mess
and the sour scent of skin
gone days without bathing.
I needed help and the head nurse sent you,
not much taller than I,
decades younger, gentle-voiced,
brown-faced with a sweet smile.

You half lifted me into the shower,
turned the spigots on, wet my hair,
poured out shampoo, lathered that tangled mass,
rinsed and conditioned it til the snarls fell free.
Then, gently cradling me in your strong arms,
you lathered me, and poured over my broken self
the healing waters of your tender care.

I was still hobbled, but for that moment, revived,
and made briefly beautiful,
whole and alive in a stranger's eyes.

I Didn't Mean to Forget

That tree outside my window
with broad leaves
and blowsy pink blossoms,
their taut centers swirled open —
its April beauty stuns
but its name eludes me,
balancing on the edge of memory
like a dogwood bloom
on an arched limb.

Something else tugs at my heart:
a lover as vivid as this fuchsia
centered on the table, but his name
gone gone gone with that tree,
its petals an opaque veil
over so much I can't say.

Still Waiting

the dead know what they are doing
they attend classes in forgetting
and come out with diplomas of silence
— Richard Shelton, *Prophets*

Where is that word I want you to speak?
Does grief become another stone,
hard and silent, dumb as this wound
carried for years and turned
into a mouth stitched shut?

Climb up death's spine,
rattle the coins you saved for Charon.
Do not forget, do not forget:
send word from the River Styx.

Encore

I believe souls come back.
My mother a green-throated Anna
hovering at the hummingbird feeder,
or a deer with her fawn
beneath the apple tree
in moonlight.

My father, crippled by Parkinson's,
wanted to become
a succession of quick things:
the lizard, still as a stick on the walkway,
then the lightning slither into shrubs,
the last flick of tail.

Braiding

Give yourself to air, to what you cannot hold.
— Rainer Maria Rilke, *Sonnets to Orpheus, Part 1, IV*

Beyond the browning pasture with the colt
and pinto mare, side-by-side,
past the hoof-heavy field
where Holsteins lump together
in the thin shade of an autumn oak,
cradled in the mountain-ringed valley,
a cemetery swallows the bones
of mother, father, and taut-tongued ancestors.

Mist swirls and my mother
wakes in gold sunrise,
dances slowly around the graves.
I yearn to slip into her phantom arms,
an ephemeral wisp around me.
Even when I cannot hold her,
I am held.

Subterranean Spring

Maybe you are searching among the branches
for what only appears in the roots.
— Rumi

A bucketful of twisting limbs —
apricot, peach and plum —
with buds ripe for opening.

No soil to sustain them,
only water, but they thrive,
flower on the twigs.

In dark neglect, deeper than the spade can dig,
against all odds, the heart roots
and dares to bloom.

The Secret Behind Mona Lisa's Smile

I'm shopping in Safeway when I find
a torn sheet of heart-ringed stationery
on the olive oil shelf.
At the bottom of the pencil-scribbled list
of food items is a note in impossible-to-miss
DayGlow fluorescent pink:

amazing how alive being touched, loved, treasured, kissed
makes me/you/anyone feel. Possibly the path to world peace
if only we universally pursue it — Diana

I glance around but see only a young guy
in a blue apron stocking balsamic vinegar.
While I shop I keep looking for a mysterious woman
radiating quiet bliss. Perhaps I'll find her
wandering down the pasta aisle,
or comparing labels on twenty brands of yogurt.
Maybe she'll be in the fruit and vegetable section.
I know I'll recognize her. She'll be the one
bending over a bin of mangoes
and glowing.

After Phillip Moved

I miss Phillip's loud voice
boomeranging over the oleanders, his laugh gusting
like a late-March wind. I miss his truck
belching in reverse with its defective muffler.

He cussed and spit, and hunted the fields
when he wasn't driving his company's CAT
down a precipitous hill.
Live on the edge, his motto. No excuses
for foul language or bold tattoos.

I kept a healthy distance until I discovered
he believed neighbors stuck together.
He raised hell, but he'd raise a roof, too.

I miss Phillip. I even miss his tattoos.

Mid-Life Blackout

Forget your perfect offering.
There is a crack in everything.
That's how the light gets in.
                    — Leonard Cohen

You're boxing yourself into shadows,
decoupaging darkness
over every window. Even the crack
beneath the door is stuffed with rags.

Punch through those papier-mâché walls;
grasp that glimmer of light.
My heart is a piñata
meant to break open.

Apple

If this was Adam's last kiss,
how fitting it should be
beneath this fringe of trees,
a primitive paradise
of light and lake and deep woods,

his mouth tasting
as tangy and sweet
as the first apple
of autumn
he had just eaten,

not a trace
of bitterness in it.

Another Chance

Something needs to grab me
like Billy Goat Gruff's troll
under the bridge,

reaching for my ankle
and pulling me down into a morass
I don't understand,

giving me a second lifetime
to figure it out.

A Condensed History

The days are gymnasts tumbling
over each other, gathering
into months, heaping into years.

We just got here. Time to go.
All those questions
still poised on our lips —
acrobats that never leaped.

About the Author

Christine Vovakes, winner of the 2018 Blue Light Poetry Prize, lives in northern California. *The Cape Rock, San Pedro River Review, Carrying the Branch: Poets in Search of Peace, Poetry Breakfast, Aethlon Journal of Sports Literature, California Quarterly, JAMA, Eclectica, Boston Literary Magazine, Watershed, Apple Valley Review, Shamrock Haiku Journal* and the *Marin Poetry Center Anthology* are among the publications where her poems have appeared. Her articles and photos have been published in *The Washington Post, Christian Science Monitor, Sacramento Bee* and *San Francisco Chronicle*. Her short story won a Patricia Painton Scholarship at the 2005 Paris Writers Workshop.

www.ingramcontent.com/pod-product-compliance
Lightning Source LLC
Chambersburg PA
CBHW021918040426

42447CB00007B/912